Sports Illustrated Kids: Legend vs. Legend

SERENA WILLIAMS VS. VENUS WILLIAMS

TENNIS LEGENDS FACE OFF

by Karen Bischer

CAPSTONE PRESS
a capstone imprint

Published by Capstone Press, an imprint of Capstone
1710 Roe Crest Drive, North Mankato, Minnesota 56003
capstonepub.com

Library of Congress Cataloging-in-Publication Data is available on the Library of Congress website.

ISBN: 9781669079781 (hardcover)
ISBN: 9781669079736 (paperback)
ISBN: 9781669079743 (ebook PDF)

Summary: Serena and Venus Williams are tennis superstars! Between the two, Serena has more career aces, but Venus has clocked the fastest serve. So which one is the all-time best? Young readers can decide for themselves by comparing the fantastic feats and stunning stats of two legendary pro tennis players.

Editorial Credits
Editor: Christopher Harbo; Designer: Sarah Bennett; Media Researcher: Svetlana Zhurkin; Production Specialist: Katy LaVigne

Image Credits
Getty Images: Al Bello, 23, Allsport/Clive Brunskill, 9, Allsport/Matthew Stockman, 15, Andy Lyons, 26, Clive Brunskill, cover (left), 11, 19, 20, 22, Hannah Peters, 24, Harry How, 12, Ian Walton, 16, Julian Finney, cover (right), Matthew Stockman, 8, Mike Stobe, 7, Quinn Rooney, 21, Robert Prezioso, 17, Ron C. Angle, 6, Scott Barbour, 14, Vince Bucci, 27, Warren Little, 25; Shutterstock: action sports, 29, hinnamsaisuy, 28, jctabb, 5, Leonard Zhukovsky, 4, 13, Neale Cousland, 10, saicle (background), cover and throughout

Printed in the United States 6278

CONTENTS

** * * All stats are current through July 2023. * * **

Words in **bold** appear in the glossary.

Tennis Legends Face Off!

Venus and Serena Williams aren't just sisters. They are two of the greatest tennis players of all time! Serena is known for her power and success on hard surfaces. Venus has a bold style and plays well on grass courts. Which one is the best? Let's find out!

Serena Williams

THE MATCHUP	Born	State
Serena	September 26, 1981	Michigan
Venus	June 17, 1980	California

Number-One Rankings

Pro tennis players earn points when they win **matches**. In 2002, Venus became the first Black woman to top the **WTA** standings. She spent 11 weeks at number one during her **career**. A few months later, Serena took the top spot. During her career, she spent 319 weeks at number one!

Venus was ranked number-one in the WTA for the first time in February 2002.

Serena posing with one of her WTA number-one trophies

THE MATCHUP	WTA No. 1 Player
Venus	11 weeks
Serena	319 weeks

Match Win Streaks

Winning one pro tennis match isn't easy. Winning dozens in a row is amazing! In 2013, Serena won 34 matches in a row. But Venus just beats her out. In 2000, she won 35 straight matches!

Serena celebrates her win in a 2013 WTA championship.

Venus raises her trophy after winning a championship in 2000.

THE MATCHUP	Matches Won in a Row
Serena	34
Venus	35

Fastest Serves

Both Venus and Serena have powerful serves. Serena's top clocked speed was 128.6 miles (206.96 kilometers) per hour in 2013. In 2007, Venus hit a 129-mile (207.61-km) per hour serve. She did it again in 2008 in a match against her sister!

Serena prepares to serve during the 2013 Australian Open.

Venus serves during the 2007 US Open.

THE MATCHUP	Fastest Serves
Serena	128.6 miles (206.96 km) per hour
Venus	129 miles (207.61 km) per hour

Most Aces in a Year

With their strong serves, Venus and Serena are **ace** experts! The WTA started recording service stats in 2008. Since then, Serena's top year for aces was 2015. She had 498. Venus's best year was 2009 with 277 aces.

Venus serving during a match at a BNP Paribas Open

Serena delivering a powerful serve at an Australian Open match

THE MATCHUP	Most Aces in a Year
Serena	498
Venus	277

Major Tournament Wins

Every tennis player wants to win **Grand Slam** events. They include the Australian Open, the French Open, the US Open, and Wimbledon. Serena has 23 Grand Slam event titles. She has won each of them at least three times. Venus won the US Open twice and Wimbledon five times.

Serena celebrates her winning point at the Australian Open.

Venus holding one of her US Open trophies

THE MATCHUP	Grand Slam Event Titles
Serena	23
Venus	7

Grand Slam Double Bagels

Hold the cream cheese! A **double bagel** isn't a breakfast food in tennis. It's when a player wins a match with two 6–0 sets. Venus has had two double bagel matches in Grand Slam events. Serena has had four Grand Slam double bagels.

Venus playing in a double bagel match at Wimbledon in 2015

Serena won a match with two 6–0 sets during the 2013 Australian Open.

THE MATCHUP	Grand Slam Double Bagels	Events
Venus	2	2002 US Open 2015 Wimbledon
Serena	4	2003 French Open 2012 US Open 2013 Australian Open 2013 US Open

Olympic Medals

Venus and Serena are both Olympic champions. Playing together, they have taken home three gold medals in **doubles** matches. But that's not all. Venus has a **singles** gold and a **mixed doubles** silver. Serena has a singles gold too.

THE MATCHUP	Olympics Medals
Venus	5
Serena	4

Venus (left) and Serena celebrate their 2008 Olympic gold medals for women's doubles.

Lowest Seeding Wins

As great as they are, both sisters have sometimes been underdogs. Venus has won two Grand Slam event titles when she wasn't ranked as a top-10 player. In 2005, she won at Wimbledon as a 14 **seed**. In 2007, she won there again as a 23 seed. In 2007, Serena wasn't even seeded when she won the Australian Open!

Venus celebrates her victory at Wimbledon in 2007.

Serena poses with her 2007 Australian Open trophy.

THE MATCHUP	Lowest Seeding Grand Slam Win
Venus	2 Wimbledon titles as a double-digit seed
Serena	1 Australian Open title with no seeding

Career Records

Both sisters have won a ton of matches! Serena's all-time record is 858 wins and 156 losses. Venus has 818 wins and 276 losses. Against each other in competitions, Serena is 19–12 over Venus.

Venus (right) congratulates Serena on her win at Wimbledon.

Venus celebrates winning a match against Serena.

THE MATCHUP	Match Records	Head-to-Head Wins in Competitions
Serena	858–156	19
Venus	818–276	12

Career Earnings

Prize money plays a big part in pro tennis. Serena won an incredible $94,816,730 in her career. Venus has also been super successful, winning $42,513,897. They are the top two all-time prize winners in women's tennis!

Serena celebrating her win at New Zealand's ASB Classic

Venus with one of her WTA championship trophies

THE MATCHUP	Career Earnings
Serena	$94,816,730
Venus	$42,513,897

Awards

Venus and Serena have won a lot of awards! Both sisters have been named WTA Player of the Year. Venus has won it once. Serena has won it seven times. They've also racked up Best Female Tennis Player ESPY awards. Venus has three. Serena has 10.

Serena holding one of her WTA Player of the Year awards

Venus poses with one of her Best Female Tennis Player ESPY awards.

THE MATCHUP	WTA Player of the Year Awards	Best Female Tennis Player ESPYs
Venus	1	3
Serena	7	10

Who Is the Best Player?

Venus and Serena are queens of the tennis court. Venus was ranked number one first, but Serena has more weeks at the top. Serena has oodles of aces, but Venus has a faster serve. Both have outplayed **opponents** and wowed fans with their grit and flair.

Who is the best player? You make the call!

Venus Williams

Serena Williams

Glossary

ace (AYSS)—a serve in tennis that is not returned, or even touched, by the other player

career (kuh-REER)—a person's main work over a large part of their life

double bagel (DUH-buhl BAY-guhl)—a tennis match won with scores of 6-0, 6-0

doubles (DUH-buhls)—two teams of two players competing in one match

Grand Slam (GRAND SLAM)—relating to the four major pro tennis tournaments, including the Australian Open, French Open, US Open, and Wimbledon

match (MACH)—a tennis contest consisting of games and sets

mixed doubles (MIKST DUH-buhls)—two teams each made up of one man and one woman who compete against each other

opponent (uh-POH-nuhnt)—a person who competes against another person

seed (SEED)—the number a player is ranked in a tournament

singles (SING-guhls)—two players competing against each other in a match

WTA (DUB-uhl-yu TEE AY)—short for the Women's Tennis Association

Read More

Leslie, Jay. *Game, Set, Sisters!: The Story of Venus and Serena Williams.* New York: Henry Holt and Company, 2021.

Nelson, Kristen Rajczak. *Serena Williams: Tennis GOAT.* Buffalo, NY: Gareth Stevens Publishing, 2024.

Wiener, Gary. *Serena vs. Venus vs. Sharapova vs Navratilova.* New York: Rosen Publishing, 2020.

Internet Sites

Kiddle: Venus Williams Facts for Kids
kids.kiddle.co/Venus_Williams

The Official Home of the Women's Tennis Association
wtatennis.com

Time for Kids: The Greatest
timeforkids.com/g34/the-greatest-g3/?rl=en-700

Index

About the Author

Photo by K. Bischer

Karen Bischer is a writer and New Jersey resident who loves watching sports, especially baseball. When she's not cheering on her beloved New York Yankees, you can find her playing with (or being bossed around by) her cat, Clarence, and dog, Brandy.